WEDGWOOD BLUE, 1979

WEDGWOOD BLUE, 1979

SEVEN, 1979

4

SEVEN, 1979

This publication was originated on
the occasion of the exhibition
at Barbican Art Gallery, London
February, 1992

KENYA, 1980

WILLIAM EGGLESTON
ANCIENT AND MODERN

Introduction by Mark Holborn

RANDOM HOUSE
NEW YORK

At home, 1978

William Eggleston was driving with the writer Stanley Booth from Georgia to Tennessee. It was 1978 and Eggleston had acquired an early Kodak instant camera. He started to photograph out of the window of the car and pointed the camera at the sky. The small, rectangular colour prints looked to him like fragments of frescoes. The following day he lay back on the ground and looked up at the sky above him. At the zenith he found a heightened clarity. However dramatic the skies then appeared towards the horizon, he imposed upon himself the constant discipline of photographing directly upwards. He was excited by the touches of blue between the clouds and by the intensity of the light. His attitude was one of exploration. He applied his methodical discipline to the quality of blue. Eggleston combines precision with delicacy.

The sky, loaded with romantic connotation and celestial symbolism, had been the subject of Stieglitz's 'Equivalent' photographs in the Twenties and Thirties. Stieglitz placed his highest aspiration in these photographs, which were small, concentrated prints, suggestive of vast scale. The points of light they contained were surrounded by dark, nocturnal clouds. Eggleston was fully aware of the pictures but made no allusion to them. He was grounded in the ordinary, fascinated by the mundane. The touches of blue revealed a stronger debt to painting than to photography. He began to use a 6 x 9 cm. Mamiya rangefinder camera and produced several hundred prints of the sky. He titled the series *Wedgwood Blue*. At the same time he began to photograph the tops of trees and in search of denser vegetation and more exotic flora, he set off for Africa.

Eggleston was born and raised in the South. He has lived all his life between Mississippi and Memphis. His reputation is built on the small portion of his work that has been published or exhibited over the last fifteen years. Much of that work would suggest that he could be described as a Southern artist, an identity he is anxious to avoid. The South is the central axis of his life, the sense of locality is a vital component of his work, but it is not defined by a Southern domain. He travels frequently and explores a wider world. If one were to construct a portrait of him, he would be sitting on a porch polishing a gun or fingering a Leica – and he is explicit on the association between the two – or else he would be behind the wheel of a car, though driving seems to have little to do with transportation and much more to do with the rhythm and pattern of his observation. He is an explorer and a resident of the South.

Driving with him into the heart of the Mississippi Delta he is expansive about his roots. 'This is Eggleston country,' he exclaims, with a wave across an immeasurable horizon as he points out a ruined plantation house or an empty site where family once lived. The signs off Highway 61 are resonant with the history of the blues. This is the land of Muddy Waters, or names as evocative as Lake Cormorant, where Son House recorded in the Forties. Eggleston land bordered on the territory of Parchman Farm, the prison about which Bukka White sang so poignantly. Eggleston later knew Bukka in Memphis, but he entered the juke joints of the Delta only occasionally as a child. He was busy learning Bach. It is precisely his knowledge of the very heart of the Delta, coupled with the cultivated European sensibility of an educated Southern background, that informs both the rawness and the sheer lyricism of his work. The combination enables him to delve in the dirt and also amongst the flowers. Recently on such a drive, heading down Highway 61 for Greenwood, I noticed a storm gathering. The sky blackened and a shower broke to our east over the river. Shafts of light cut diagonals across the huge sky in biblical fashion. It was then clear how that landscape, the intensity of that plain, produced skies of immense drama. An imagination nurtured on such a view might be deeply impressed by a sense of space and by the colour of frescoes, of blues between the painted clouds.

William Eggleston's stated biographical facts are that he was born in Memphis in 1939 and brought up on the family cotton farm in Tallahatchie County, Mississippi. He went to school in Sumner, Mississippi and in Tennessee. He says he occasionally attended Vanderbilt University, Delta State College and the University of Mississippi. He acquired his first camera, a Canon rangefinder in 1957, followed by his first Leica in 1958. His only source of photographs was in the popular magazines of the Fifties, until around 1960, when he saw copies of Walker Evans's *American Photographs* (1938) and Henri Cartier-Bresson's *The Decisive Moment* (1952). He still returns to Cartier-Bresson, but there are few books on his shelves. In his private world, William Klein's *Tokyo* (1964) is conspicuous amidst albums of baroque music, books on the architecture of Berlin and catalogues of audio equipment and firearms. He rarely talks about the work of other photographers, though he remains emphatic in his admiration for the work of his friends Lee Friedlander and Gary Winogrand.

In Lincoln Kirstein's essay accompanying Walker Evans's *American Photographs* he indicated the collective nature of the sequence as opposed to isolated, individual prints, 'Looked at in sequence they are overwhelming in their exhaustiveness of detail, their poetry of contrast, and, for those who wish to see it, their moral implication'. He described Evans's eye as 'elevating the casual, the everyday and the literal into specific, permanent symbols'. The flow of such imagery created an unprecedented vision of 'the contemporary civilization of eastern America and its dependencies'.

Evans had made plain the facts of the street, the house, the wall, the architectural detail, the automobile, and by focusing on the presence of objects he transformed the ordinary with a clarity that was extraordinary. The understated observation then acquired the grandeur of coherent vision. The catalogue for Evans's exhibition at The Museum of Modern Art, New York, prepared by John Szarkowski in 1971, four years before Walker Evans's death, opened with a quotation from Whitman:

> I do not doubt but the majesty and beauty of the world are latent in any iota of the world . . .
> I do not doubt there is far more in trivialities, insects, vulgar persons, slaves, dwarfs, weeds, rejected refuse, than I have supposed . . .

Following in the wake of Stieglitz's elevated aspiration, the lesson of Evans's work was rooted in a vernacular language, grounding the viewer with a common poetry. It was to form a dominant tradition, through the epic of Robert Frank's *The Americans* (1959), and was to remain prevalent for at least another fifty years. Its influence on Eggleston would have been inescapable.

The strategy that Walker Evans employed was directness. The revelations came from the straight line of sight, head-on. Evans's view of the South, especially along the back roads of Alabama, increased a sense of the flattening of the architectural facades, the signage and the posters. One becomes conscious of the two dimensions of the planes as if he had stretched the design of the photograph like a canvas to expose the geometry of its form. With careful respect for Evans, Eggleston began to regard this frontal purity of style as if it was a formula he wanted to break. 'If there was anything about Walker Evans's work that I disliked', he said, 'it was his determination always to use that same, square, frontal view. I never cared much for any photographs with such frontal fields.'

In Cartier-Bresson, Eggleston found a new elastic device. 'His were the first pictures I'd seen which weren't just straight-on pictures like everybody else's. He had angles like Degas or Toulouse-Lautrec – one picture after another. I think I understood Evans, but my real discovery was Cartier-Bresson.'

Eggleston's early black and white photographs show all the influence of *The Decisive Moment* and the fluidity the Leica granted. Angles and diagonals proliferate. The book impressed him on account of the luminosity of the French gravure printing. He was more fascinated with the tonal range of the plates than with the images depicted and he later admitted to disappointment on seeing the actual prints, which appeared to him like ordinary photographs,

devoid of the delicacy of the gravure. In the second half of the book, devoted to Asia, is a photograph from France, taken in 1946, which lies adjacent to views of Peking yet remains wholly congruous. It shows in softened and diffuse tones a row of winter trees and gardens in a village on the Loire near Blois. Eggleston described it as an 'oriental' view and saw it as he would a Japanese screen. It appealed to a feminine, lyrical side of his sensibility, which would later surface in his own work with such elegance.

In Amory, Mississippi in 1966 Eggleston photographed an interior by pointing up at the floral wallpaper, mirror and light-fitting of the room at such an angle that he broke the customary frontal plane yet intensified the sense of abstraction. He rearranged the space of the rectangle of the photograph with diagonals. It was clear that he was not engaged in an act of illustration but was discovering his own language. His sense of the frame is immaculately precise. Out of the most ordinary situation he had found the raw material for his work. He had developed a photographic prototype. At the same time he was examining the technical limitations of the film itself. He pointed the camera in a later photograph straight up at the ceiling, centering on an illuminated chandelier, forcefully overexposing the negative to find the desired tonal effect. The most common perspective was of course the surprising view, one that might be contemplated from a bed or a bath or if one was outstretched on the floor. It was in the ordinary rhythms of daily life that he made the most radical departures.

In 1965 and 1966 he began experimenting with colour negative film. An early print of a gas station echoed Evans

HOLLY SPRINGS, MISSISSIPPI, 1963

LUNCH, 1963

15

in its subject, yet flamboyantly depicted the colour with a range of reds, blues and yellows, including the red of rust, which Eggleston subsequently played down. Rust later became almost part of the 'Southern' language, especially through the work of Eggleston's friend, William Christenberry, who he had known for more than twenty years, and whose relationship with Walker Evans is well documented. Christenberry's work is exclusively Southern, being derived from his home country of Hale County, Alabama, the location of Agee's and Evans's masterpiece *Let Us Now Praise Famous Men* (1941). Christenberry was a painter and sculptor for whom the corroded signs of Alabama were his raw material. Rust was the dominant colour of his spectrum. His exquisite early photographic studies, championed by Walter Hopps in 1969 and by Walker Evans in 1972, his sculptural work and his later large prints were an overt inheritance of the Evans legacy. Eggleston began to underplay the obvious categorisation of his work as a further extension of any Southern school.

In the late Sixties Eggleston turned to the use of colour transparency film and photographed prolifically. He visited New York with suitcases of work and sought out Winogrand, Friedlander and Diane Arbus. He was advised to show his photographs to John Szarkowski at The Museum of Modern Art, who immediately recognised the strength of the work. 'When I went to see John at MoMA,' Eggleston said, 'I had suitcases of early slides and some prints, including some early black and white. I had to leave them at the museum and come back the next day like everybody else. He invited me in and I was greatly thrilled and relieved by his response. I had no idea what he was going to say. I was very impatient. I wanted to get my work out into the world and he encouraged me to be patient.' The meeting was the beginning of the process which was to lead to his exhibition and the accompanying book *William Eggleston's Guide* in May 1976. It is now regarded as a significant date, since it marks the acceptance of colour photography by the highest validating institution. Colour was no longer 'vulgar' as Walker Evans had once claimed. It had become a legitimate mode of photographic expression, transcending its previous purely commercial application. At the time, the show was greeted with considerable controversy.

The exhibition was based on work shot on transparency film between 1969 and 1971. Eggleston and Szarkowski wanted to make the work cohesive, so they drew from a single body of about four hundred slides, ignoring the earlier colour negative work. They selected down to one hundred photographs, then finally hung seventy-five prints. Between the time the photographs were taken and their eventual exhibition, Eggleston made significant technical advances including his first experiments with video technology. While teaching at Harvard in 1973 and 1974 he had discovered dye-transfer printing. 'I was reading the price list of this lab in Chicago and it advertised "from the cheapest to the ultimate print". The ultimate print was a dye-transfer. I went straight up there to look and everything I saw was commercial work like pictures of cigarette packs or perfume bottles but the colour saturation and the quality of the ink was overwhelming. I couldn't wait to see what a plain Eggleston picture would look like with the same process. Every photograph I subsequently

WEBB, MISSISSIPPI, 1964

printed with the process seemed fantastic and each one seemed better than the previous one.'

'I don't think anything has the seductivity of dyes,' Eggleston once said, 'I've always said that a dye is not better, it's just different. I'm tempted to say that a C-print (chromogenic coupler print) is more faithful than a dye. It's not as dramatic. By the time you get into all those dyes, it doesn't look at all like the scene, which in some cases is what you want.'*

The first dyes he had made were of the image of Greenwood Moose Lodge, a sombre, windowless edifice against a blue sky, and *The Red Ceiling* in 1973. He was so impressed with them that he knew dye-transfers were going to provide him with his medium. He immediately sent Szarkowski a print of *The Red Ceiling*, which was to become one of his most famous images. The cross of white cable leading to the potent, central light bulb, was what he described as a 'fly's eye view' in the guest room of his friend, a dentist in Greenwood, Mississippi, whose choice of décor included an adjacent blue room; he can be seen naked, his walls daubed with graffiti, in *The Guide*. The house with the red room was subsequently burned down and his friend murdered, yet far from having any sinister connotation, the red room was immensely pleasing to Eggleston. 'The Red Ceiling is so powerful, that in fact I've never seen it reproduced on the page to my satisfaction,' Eggleston claimed. 'When you look at the dye it is like red blood that's wet on the wall. The photograph was like a Bach exercise for me because I knew that red was the most difficult colour to work with. A little red is usually enough, but to work with an entire red surface was a challenge. It was hard to do.

I don't know of any totally red pictures, except in advertising. The photograph is still powerful. It shocks you every time.'

While at Harvard he prepared his first portfolio, simply titled *14 Pictures* (1974), containing fourteen dye-transfers, which he regards as one of the best groupings of his work. The colour was forceful. The pictures were astonishing for their strange angles and their unusual subject matter. The work was far too radical to be considered pretty. The portfolio included a photograph of a grave at night with the word 'Father' caught in the flash. It was taken from ground level, in the grass. Another picture included a group of brightly coloured toy animals on a black background, seen as if arranged by a child. The strangest view was of clutter and old shoes shot from beneath a bed. When I asked him how the picture came about, he replied, 'I was just exploring.'

Before the museum exhibition and the publication of *The Guide*, Eggleston had returned to using negative film because he could purposefully overexpose it. This he often did by changing the ASA rating of the film contrary to the specifications Kodak provided. Between 1967 and 1974 he completed a vast series of over two thousand photographs. With the money he received from a Guggenheim Fellowship in 1974 he printed up the project and titled it *Los Alamos* after visiting the nuclear test site in New Mexico. The work was made on his travels from Memphis through the Delta, to New Orleans, Southern California and Las Vegas. It remained unseen until Walter Hopps recently published eight of the photographs in *Grand Street*. Hopps

*Carole Thompson, 'William Eggleston: Seen & Unseen', The Print Collector's Newsletter, vol xx, 1–5, November/December 1990

wrote that '... the lengthy span of images from these travels was for him something like a fragment of a novel – a sympathetic viewer could not avoid bringing some narrative order, however disjunctive, to the sequence.'★ The excursions, radiating out from his axis of Memphis and the Delta, together with the scale of the project, served as precedents for his epic of the Eighties, *The Democratic Forest*.

Although Eggleston had moved on to new work at the time of the museum exhibition, for the public it was a completely different experience. Not only was colour new in a museum context, but dye-transfers were an unknown medium. Hilton Kramer was scathing in *The New York Times* (May 28, 1976), 'To this snapshot style, Mr Eggleston has added some effects borrowed from recent developments in of all things – photo-realist painting – a case, if not of the blind leading the blind, at least the banal leading the banal.' 'Snapshot' and 'banal' became the buzz words of hostility, despite Szarkowski's reference to the inherent structure of the work. It was Kramer, who only a year before, had written that Walker Evans was one of the greatest artists of his generation. Eggleston he believed was an 'anti-formalist'. In his introduction to *The Guide*, Szarkowski drew attention to the circular core of many of the pictures, which radiated out to the frame – a pattern clearly demonstrated by *The Red Ceiling* – 'Just like the Confederate flag,' Eggleston had responded.

The Guide excluded several important pictures that were in the show. The tone of the book might have been disrupted by such drama as *The Red Ceiling*. The sequence, starting with the front door, is a very low-key introduction to Eggleston's world. Its subjects are, on the surface, the ordinary inhabitants and environs of suburban Memphis and Mississippi – friends, family, barbeques, back yards, a tricycle and the clutter of the mundane. The normality of these subjects is deceptive, for behind the images there is a sense of lurking danger. The work might well have set a precedent for David Lynch's film *Blue Velvet* (1989), where the evidence of evil is hidden in the grass beside the sprinklers of suburban lawns, and where the emotional weight of the film is so dependent on the formal ingredients of colour and angle. Lynch's camera descended into the grass itself. Eggleston's 'insect eye', which probed into the heart of the mundane, or as Eudora Welty suggested made a cross-cut through the grain of the ordinary to the very centre, was dismissed bitterly at the time of the exhibition.†

The Guide was very concise. Eggleston's sense of scale had increased with the vast *Los Alamos* project. The idea of a series emphasised an even hierarchy of imagery rather than a collection of single, virtuoso photographs. On the eve of Carter's election in the fall of 1976, Eggleston drove to Plains, Georgia, on assignment for *Rolling Stone*. He came back with meticulous photographs of roads and the plainest, understated landscape. He recently disclosed that it was on this journey that he first abandoned the use of a viewfinder on the camera. He began to shoot as if he was firing a shotgun. 'It makes you much freer, so you can hold the camera up in the air as if you were ten feet tall. You end up looking more intensely as you walk around. When it is time for you to make the photograph, it's all ready for you. Unlike a rifle, where you carefully aim following a dot or a scope, with a shotgun it's done with feel. You don't look down the barrel and line things up. With a fluid movement

★*Grand Street 36*, New York, 1990   †Eudora Welty, Introduction to *The Democratic Forest*, London and New York, 1989

your body follows a moving target and the gun keeps moving after the shot with what is known as 'follow through'. That becomes subconscious. Good shooting instructors will encourage you to follow through. It's the opposite of the rational method. When I got the prints from this method, they looked like shotgun pictures.'

The Georgia work from 6 x 9 cm. negatives was bound into two large volumes containing one hundred prints in an edition of five. This ambitious enterprise undertaken by Caldecot Chubb was based on *Gardner's Sketchbook of the Civil War* (1866) and was titled *Election Eve* (1977). The book became an ideal form for seeing Eggleston's work and Chubb subsequently produced three further exquisite Eggleston volumes, *Morals of Vision* (1978) and *Flowers* (1978), culminating in *Wedgwood Blue* (1979), which contained fifteen of his cloud prints bound in blue silk. The elegance of these productions matched the delicacy of the work.

Eggleston's interest in video had resulted in several hours of black and white tape which he refers to as *Stranded in Canton* (1973 and 1974). The video camera provided the tool for recording a continuous flow of events, as if all observations were of equivalent significance before the lens. The roots of his ideas of a 'democratic' camera were developing. He was also familiar with Warhol's world and was spending time at the Chelsea Hotel where he had a long relationship with Warhol's superstar Viva. Warhol's neutral gaze and the endless possibility of his films increased the sense of the camera observer before whom the world of extreme diversity or mundanity simply unfolds.

Eggleston had become friends with Richard Leacock, the pioneer of video, in the early Sixties. He had later joined Leacock in Louisiana to work on a film of Walker Percy's novel *The Moviegoer*, which was eventually abandoned. In 1978 he was asked by Leacock to join him at the Massachusetts Institute of Technology to investigate the possibilities of colour video. His video experiments affected his photographic attitude. He wanted to make photographs in which he almost abdicated his role as photographer and operated as if he were an unmanned probe scanning the world for evidence without distinction. Like an extraterrestrial eye he could view his surroundings without selecting suitable subject matter. Everything constituted evidence. This liberating principle was practised during a commission he received at the time from the American Telephone and Telegraph Company (1978), for whom he photographed the landscape, flora and vegetation of the Gulf states. 'These photographs were taken along the thirty-second parallel, where the southeastern coastal plain begins to be tropical. They're related in concept to a particular video piece I've been doing that's something like an unmanned probe, in that the camera travels along a certain path at a certain pace and produces information about whatever might be found there. The photographs are not meant to be "romantic" nor to be about the South.'* In the same year he travelled to Jamaica and photographed vegetation and the flowers of the Caribbean.

The collaboration with Caldecot Chubb continued with the publication of *Seven* (1979) containing seven C-prints of trees and foliage, in which he filled the frame with the pattern of branches. This appeared at the time of *Wedgwood Blue* and shared some of the same stance, an upward gaze at the sky. Together they went to Kenya where he photographed the soil, the flowers and trees, often from ground level. He was becoming geological in his concerns. 'When I got to Kenya, it dawned on me that everything I was seeing was the result of violent volcanic activity aeons ago,' he explained. 'Almost every big, round stone in the middle of nowhere had been hurled hundreds of miles by terrific explosions and the two great mountains, Kilimanjaro and Mount Kenya, were built. I tried to imagine what it was like when those fireballs were coming hundreds of miles. It must have been a hell of an event.'

The publication of *Troubled Waters* (1980), the last portfolio produced by Chubb, dated back to work Eggleston had selected years before while at the Chelsea Hotel when his exhibition was still hanging at the museum. It contained the image of the inside of the freezer, a counterpart to the open door of the oven from *The Guide* – both of which constitute great American interiors – but the work was distinct from his elemental images of wild landscape.

He returned to the South and began another epic series, *The Louisiana Project* (1980) in which he explored the state, combining classic views of crumbling plantation houses with burning garbage on the outskirts of New Orleans. He was finding intricate compositions in the simplest of circumstances – the surfaces of walls, a row of steps, amidst dereliction and graveyards, then out on the road across great sweeping vistas of the landscape of this Southern heartland. The publication of another portfolio of dyes, *Southern Suite* (1981) further suggested the image of the Southern artist with photographs of the freight train on the

Delta horizon, a Delta railroad-crossing in the early morning and the first dye-transfer, the Greenwood Moose Lodge. Meanwhile the African and Caribbean work remained unknown.

A surprising invitation followed in 1981 to photograph the sets for John Huston's film *Annie* (1982) which was being shot in a mansion in New Jersey that had been built for the president of F. W. Woolworth in 1928. The invitation was extended to a number of photographers including Gary Winogrand. Eggleston found it impossible to work surrounded by the intense activity of a film crew, but he returned to the mansion when they were finished. He produced a remarkable series of interiors, in which he moved close to the surface of the walls and pointed upwards as he had in the open landscape. The most surprising shot was up at a large panel of many light switches, which he had photographed from Annie's view of the daunting vastness of the mansion. The other photographers were engaged in illustrating the film-set, Eggleston had adopted the perception of a child.

This single interior shot opened up exactly what Eggleston's strange angles demonstrated. The enigmatic photograph of a tricycle on the cover of *The Guide* was clearly a child's view from the ground. The psychology of his 'insect's eye' and his need for the fluidity of discarding the viewfinder were now explicitly apparent. 'Sometimes I like the idea of making a picture that does not look like a human picture,' he claimed. 'Humans make pictures which tend to be about five feet above the ground looking out horizontally. I like very fast flying insects moving all over and I wonder what their view is from moment to moment.

AMORY, MISSISSIPPI, 1966

23

I have made a few pictures which show that physical viewpoint. I photographed a stuffed animal in an attempt to make a picture as if the family pet were holding a camera – from a dog or cat's view. The tricycle is similar. It is an insect's view or it could be a child's view.'

An invitation to photograph Elvis Presley's mansion, Graceland, on the outskirts of Memphis, provided the opportunity to produce his most intense dye-transfers. He established a sense of the emptiness of the house, a mausoleum inhabited by the paraphernalia of a legend. Elvis's style was excessive and colour was the language of his legend, from pink Cadillacs to blue shoes. Graceland, a euphemism for heaven, is a culmination of the great American interior. Elvis's journey from humble origins in a shack in Tupelo, Mississippi, to the house on the hill was the enactment of the American dream. Fifty years before Walker Evans had photographed the sharecroppers' interiors with all their poverty and austerity in emphatic black and white. Eggleston took on the sequel in wildly saturated colour. Several of his pictures appeared in an official guidebook to the house and the portfolio of eleven dye-transfers, *William Eggleston's Graceland* (1984) was exhibited in Washington. A pattern became evident from these commissions, as if Eggleston was constructing a grand plan. The monumental nature of Graceland, a site on his doorstep, and the scale of the portfolio itself, serves as a prefatory sign for his major undertaking of the Eighties, *The Democratic Forest*.

The democracy of Eggleston's title referred to the principle he had been applying through which everything was represented equally by the lens. He recounted its origin after photographing the undergrowth by the roadside near Holly Springs, Mississippi. 'What have you been doing today Eggleston?' someone asked. 'Photographing democratically,' he replied. The project, lasting several years, resulted in more than ten thousand prints and the publication of the book with an introduction by Eudora Welty in 1989. Since all the work has equal status in *The Democratic Forest*, it is difficult to isolate single images, though the project contains magnificent photographs. The series, not the individual prints, constitutes the work. There are recurring motifs throughout. Telephone lines and automobiles amidst foliage reappear frequently. The cables bind the world together, linking the provinces of Eggleston's territory just as the automobiles provide the transportation. He travelled from Memphis out into Tennessee and his homelands in the Delta. Lengthy chapters occur in Miami, Pittsburgh, Dallas and New Orleans and as far as the Berlin Wall. The colours range from green spring landscapes to poisonous, hallucinatory nausea in New Orleans. The book begins with a view of clouds over Mayflower County, Mississippi, his home, and ends over St Louis at night, an electric green city. His view of the world below, strung together with lines of light, is that of the modern man in motion. He always thought of the sequence as symphonic in nature with quiet passages between grand themes. Radiating out from Memphis he could explore the whole world and encompass it all within *The Democratic Forest*.

His travels continued throughout the decade and included journeys from Berlin to Vienna, Salzburg and Graz. He found modern German industrial architecture and

FLOWERS, 1978

25

the colours and signs of a reconstructed nation as suitable a subject as the patina of an ageing wall in a European city. Pinks, oranges and greys, the artificial colours of shopping streets and neon, are recurring elements in his landscape of postwar Europe. He titled the work *Kiss Me Kracow*. Following the nineteenth-century tradition of the exploratory photographer, he visited Egypt and travelled on the Nile. The familiar sepia of nineteenth-century albumen prints with views of the Pyramids and the Valley of the Kings was replaced by the burned yellow colour of Eggleston's prints, broken by touches of a brilliant blue sky. He photographed the industrial landscape of modern Egypt beside views of the ancient world. Pictures of Eggleston before he left for Egypt, show him sitting on his Memphis porch, white-suited with a gun across his lap as if he were preparing for his official portrait prior to an expedition.

In the late-Eighties he turned to painting and drawing with crayons, producing several notebooks of small, abstract works. It was as if his facility for making photographs had become too quick. Everything within his view could be accommodated and framed by the camera, and the activity was instantaneous. The drawing lasted hours through the night. It was an act of total invention in which his imagination could construct great fictions. One extended series of drawings was a description of *The Rise and Fall of the Kingdom of Kam*, an imaginary civilisation in Mesopotamia. These excursions into an invented history took place at the same time as he was photographing intricate industrial machinery, particularly the oils rigs in Tennessee. He took another international commission in 1989 and photographed factories in Toronto and England, then accepted an offer to go to the Transvaal, where he photographed both industrial plant and magnificent flora, and he could do both in the same breath. He returned several times to England and began a series of flower studies, *English Rose*. While on the streets of London, he photographed a city under massive transformation, where the historical facades were draped in tarpaulins and the buildings encased in scaffolding, the skyline broken by cranes – a landscape where the ancient and modern had collided.

His travels across Europe proceed and the stories of the man proliferate, reinforcing the Southern legend. Once on a late night search for whiskey he drove his Cadillac through locked steel gates with Bach's *Mass in B Minor* playing at full volume. There is a trail of such collisions balanced by music of mathematical order. Amidst the splintered vision of his work, there exist meticulous patterns and a discipline with which he can study flower petals or hand-guns, mansions or trash. His prodigious output has barely been seen, yet he is only in mid-stride. He continues to cut to the heart of the ordinary, probing at those things which constitute tangible dimensions, like some concrete explorer. Or, as a great exotic, he can be in the kitchen or in Zanzibar, staring at the dirt by his boot or looking up at the sky.

M.H.
August, 1991
London

MEMPHIS, *c.*1965

The Red Ceiling is so powerful that, in fact, I've never seen it reproduced on the page to my satisfaction. When you look at a dye-transfer print it's like it's red blood that is wet on the wall. The photograph was like a Bach exercise for me because I knew that red was the most difficult colour to work with. A little red is usually enough, but to work with an entire red surface was a challenge. It was hard to do. I don't know of any totally red pictures, except in advertising. The photograph is still powerful. It shocks you every time.

WILLIAM EGGLESTON

GREENWOOD, MISSISSIPPI, 1973

MEMPHIS, *c.* 1985

MEMPHIS, early 1970s

UNTITLED, 1980

33

TROUBLED WATERS, 1980

TROUBLED WATERS, 1980

THE DEMOCRATIC FOREST, 1989

To RELIGHT OVEN PILOT:
REMOVE OVEN BOTTOM BY RAISING
FRONT EDGE AND SLIDING FORWARD.
PILOT IS LOCATED AT LEFT REAR OF
BURNER LIGHT PILOT WITH A MATCH.

MEMPHIS, *c.* 1970

GREENWOOD, MISSISSIPPI *c.* 1970

SOUTHERN SUITE, 1981

14 Pictures, 1974

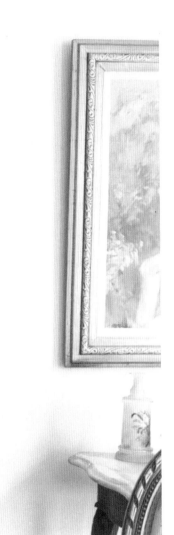

SOUTHERN SUITE, 1981

NEAR JACKSON, MISSISSIPPI, *c.* 1970

MEMPHIS, *c.* 1970

LOS ALAMOS, 1967

KENYA, 1980

Sometimes I like the idea of making a picture that does not look like a human picture. Humans make pictures which tend to be about five feet above the ground looking out horizontally. I like very fast flying insects moving all over and I wonder what their view is from moment to moment. I have made a few pictures which show that physical viewpoint. I photographed a stuffed animal in an attempt to make a picture as if the family pet were holding a camera – from a dog or cat's view.

WILLIAM EGGLESTON

WASHINGTON D.C., 1990

Near Glendora, Mississippi, *c.* 1970

Eggleston's invention is to cut from the vernacular leaving no scars, to draw from it compositions so intelligent and emotionally ingrained that they persuade us as images that weigh in at the roots of our lives. In their 'commonness' they achieve the peace that comes from a sense of absolute belonging, hence their spell.

Using processed color with the modulation, the sense of even habit, with which a genre painter, a Chardin, used painted color (also to depict 'the commonplace'), he has found a way for light to have air in color, to breathe from it instead of be blocked by it – as usually happens in color photography. The color is so in key with Eggleston's vision of his subject, so matter-of-fact, that one could slip into not thinking about it. But it is the big wave on which all the information rides in. For example, the red-and-black-striped necktie, which was taken at a relative's funeral, is the wise blood of a picture sucking up color in its thorough dedication to the history of the subject of black and white (photography and people).

INGRID SISCHY
extract from *Artforum*, February 1983

SUMNER, MISSISSIPPI, CASSIDY BAYOU, 1971

Bill Eggleston's stuff sure didn't strike me at first as 'good' photography. I mean, everything isn't always in focus, the 'subject' isn't always in the center (it's sometimes chopped off!) and the framing sure ain't what they advise in the Kodak manual. And, to top it off, unlike a lot of 'documentary' pictures, one can't even tell what some of the pictures are about. Isn't a picture supposed to be about something? Isn't it supposed to be telling us something?

But I kept going back to look at them. More and more of them. As if by staring long enough I might penetrate their mystery and understand why they mess with my mind like they do. And every time I'd think I'd uncovered some underlying system, device or technique, I'd see something else that would totally throw me for a loop.

Maybe the sensation of getting thrown for a loop is the thrill I was seeking. Like stepping off a roller-coaster, or spinning around until dizzy, or drugs, or driving music, I guess the feeling of slight disorientation is addictive.

I find these pictures very pleasantly disorienting. Some look like accidents, like somebody accidentally pressed the shutter button on the camera while examining the strap, or something. Some look like 'found' pictures ... created according to a logic that is not available to us. All ask us to re-define what we mean by beauty. Is the beauty in how they resonate? In how they make us feel? Or in how they look?

It's a world that's familiar and darkly mysterious at the same time. As if we came home one day and there was this strange smell. Unrecognizable. Well, Bill Eggleston puts that smell in there. Sweet and stinky ... but I still can't figure out what it is.

DAVID BYRNE

Untitled, 1971

57

SOUTHERN SUITE, 1981

SOUTHERN SUITE, 1981

SOUTHERN SUITE, 1981

SOUTHERN SUITE, 1981

TROUBLED WATERS, 1980

SOUTHERN SUITE, 1981

TROUBLED WATERS, 1980

TROUBLED WATERS, 1980

67

THE LOUISIANA PROJECT, 1980

THE LOUISIANA PROJECT, 1980

THE LOUISIANA PROJECT, 1980

71

THE LOUISIANA PROJECT, 1980

THE LOUISIANA PROJECT, 1980

The Louisiana Project, 1980

THE LOUISIANA PROJECT, 1980

THE LOUISIANA PROJECT, 1980

THE LOUISIANA PROJECT, 1980

THE LOUISIANA PROJECT, 1980

THE LOUISIANA PROJECT, 1980

81

If you take off the viewfinder of the camera, you end up looking more intensely as you walk around. When it is time to make the photograph it is all ready for you. If you have looked intently you know where to point the thing. This makes you much freer, so you can hold the camera up in the air as if you were ten feet tall. Unlike a rifle, where you carefully aim following a dot or a scope, with a shotgun it's done with feel. You don't look down the barrel and line things up. With a fluid movement your body follows a moving target and the gun keeps moving after the shot with what is known as 'follow through'. That becomes subconscious. Good shooting instructors will encourage you to follow through. It's the opposite of the rational method. When I got the prints from this method, they looked like shotgun pictures.

WILLIAM EGGLESTON

ELECTION EVE, 1977

ELECTION EVE, 1977

ELECTION EVE, 1977

ELECTION EVE, 1977

86

ELECTION EVE, 1977

GRACELAND, 1984

89

GRACELAND, 1984

GRACELAND, 1984

92

GRACELAND, 1984

I am afraid that there are more people than I can imagine who can go no further than appreciating a picture that is a rectangle with an object in the middle of it, which they can identify. They don't care what is around the object as long as nothing interferes with the object itself, right in the centre. Even after the lessons of Winogrand and Friedlander, they don't get it. They respect their work because they are told by respectable institutions that they are important artists, but what they really want to see is a picture with a figure or an object in the middle of it. They want something obvious. The blindness is apparent when someone lets slip the word 'snapshot'. Ignorance can always be covered by 'snapshot'. The word has never had any meaning. I am at war with the obvious.

WILLIAM EGGLESTON
The Democratic Forest

OIL RIGS, c. 1985

OIL RIGS, c. 1985

OIL RIGS, *c.* 1985

OIL RIGS, *c.*1985

OIL RIGS, *c.*1985

THE TRANSVAAL, 1989

THE TRANSVAAL, 1989

106

The Transvaal, 1989

ENGLAND, 1989

When I got to Kenya it dawned on me that everything that I was seeing was the result of volcanic violent activity aeons ago. Almost every big, round stone in the middle of nowhere had been hurled hundreds of miles by terrific explosions, and the two great mountains, Kilimanjaro and Mount Kenya, were built. I was trying to figure out what it was like when those fireballs were coming hundreds of miles. It must have been a hell of an event.

WILLIAM EGGLESTON

KENYA, 1980

III

KENYA, 1980

KENYA, 1980

114

KENYA, 1980

115

KENYA, 1980

KENYA, 1980

KENYA, 1980

KENYA, 1980

I regarded the Egypt trip as an excursion into an unknown place. I didn't seek out much beyond the typical nineteenth-century view. We travelled with an archaeologist, who would tell me in the middle of the desert that I was at the site of some ancient palace. The photographs became hazy and sepia-like because of the dust in the air. I remember the decaying ruins of recently completed modern buildings. You find yourself imagining ancient history, the scenes of a great battle or a great march, or an army of slaves passing by.

The Aswan dam has shrunken the Nile into a sad, little stream. The river was once like the Mississippi, but no one would have the audacity to dam the Mississippi. They let the Russians dam the Nile and now they should make them blow it up. The view from the boat was like paintings of Carthage – suddenly a temple would come into view like an apparition.

WILLIAM EGGLESTON

THE NILE, 1986

EGYPT, 1986

EGYPT, 1986

125

EGYPT, 1986

127

EGYPT, 1986

128

EGYPT, 1986

EGYPT, 1986

EGYPT, 1986

THE TRANSVAAL, 1989

THE TRANSVAAL, 1989

THE TRANSVAAL, 1989

135

THE TRANSVAAL, 1989

THE TRANSVAAL, 1989

I was envisioning the night when people were standing and laughing as they watched the Reichstag burning. The second vision was of the Reichstag the day the Russians came in and planted the flag on top, and the building was bullet-ridden, enveloped in soot and covered with graffiti. The third view was the detail of how the bullet holes had been so meticulously, tenderly repaired.

It is an enormously handsome building on a magnificent scale. The Berliners didn't seem to care for it, as it was flanked by the Wall, which they hated. I was reminded of Speer's complete architectural statement of brutality and totalitarianism in one swoop in his design of the Chancellery, which was so powerful and well executed.

I discovered Berlin had a different spirit to the rest of Germany. There was a lightness as well as the heaviness. The photograph I made of the radiator harked back to the kinkiness of the Weimar Republic. It could have been at the back of a cabaret or in a detention room for the Gestapo.

WILLIAM EGGLESTON

THE REICHSTAG, KISS ME KRACOW, 1983–86

KISS ME KRACOW, 1983-86

KISS ME KRACOW, 1983–86

KISS ME KRACOW, 1983–86

KISS ME KRACOW, 1983-86

143

KISS ME KRACOW, 1983-86

KISS ME KRACOW, 1983-86

145

KISS ME KRACOW, 1983–86

KISS ME KRACOW, 1983-86

London still has the patina of gentility despite the modernisation, unlike Atlanta or other modern cities. I have a feeling for a secret London, which encompasses it all, from the bridges through the buildings, from Wren and Pugin to Lutyens, and to those buildings which have no architects, for which there was no design.

WILLIAM EGGLESTON

LONDON, 1989

LONDON, 1989

LONDON, 1989

151

English flowers are so English. The Englishness is crystallised in the rose, though I would like to photograph all the flowers. The English understand and need gardens. The whole work might be called *The Queen of Hearts*. About five years ago I re-discovered Max Reinhardt's film of *A Midsummer Night's Dream*, which, although it was dark, reminded me that England was a garden.

WILLIAM EGGLESTON

LONDON, 1986

CAMBRIDGE, 1986

ENGLAND, 1986

ENGLAND, 1986

158

ENGLAND, 1986

ENGLAND, 1986

ENGLAND, 1986

ENGLAND, 1986

WILLIAM EGGLESTON
CHRONOLOGY

1939   Born in Memphis, Tennessee.

1957   Acquires his first camera, a Canon rangefinder.

1958   Acquires his first Leica.

1959   Sees Henri Cartier-Bresson's *The Decisive Moment* and Walker Evans's *American Photographs*.

1965   Begins to experiment with colour transparency film.

1967   Starts to use colour negative film. Goes to New York and meets Gary Winogrand, Lee Friedlander and Diane Arbus. Presents his work to John Szarkowski at The Museum of Modern Art.

1974   Receives a Guggenheim Fellowship. Appointed Lecturer in Visual and Environmental Studies at the Carpenter Center, Harvard University. Produces his first portfolio of dye-transfer prints *14 Pictures*. Completes his *Los Alamos* project.

1975   Receives a National Endowment for the Arts Photographer's Fellowship.

1976   *William Eggleston's Guide* is published by The Museum of Modern Art, New York, to accompany a major exhibition of his dye-transfer prints, which is greeted with controversy. Commissioned by *Rolling Stone* to photograph Plains, Georgia before the election of President Jimmy Carter.

1977   *Election Eve*, two volumes of chromogenic coupler prints based on *Gardner's Sketchbook of the Civil War* is published in an edition of five by Caldecot Chubb.

1978   Appointed Researcher in Color Video at Massachusetts Institute of Technology at the invitation of Richard Leacock.

Photographs the Gulf states on a commission from A. T. & T. Receives another award from the National Endowment for the Arts. Visits Jamaica.

1980   Travels to Kenya with Caldecot Chubb and is influenced by the geology of Mount Kenya and Kilimanjaro. Commissioned to produce *The Louisiana Project* and photographs throughout the state.

1982   Invited to photograph the set of John Huston's film *Annie*.

1983   Begins to photograph in Berlin, Salzburg and Graz and titles the series *Kiss Me Kracow*. Commissioned to photograph the mansion of Elvis Presley, Graceland.

1984   Produces a portfolio of dye-transfers of Graceland.

1986   Invited by David Byrne to visit and photograph the making of his film *True Stories*. Commissioned by the Memphis Brooks Museum to photograph in Egypt.

1988   Begins a series of colour photographs of England he calls *English Rose*.

1989   *The Democratic Forest*, containing many thousands of prints, is completed and the book, with an introduction by Eudora Welty, is published in London and New York. Accepts a commercial commission to photograph industrial sites in England, Los Angeles and Toronto together with office buildings in New York and Washington. Photographs in the orange groves of The Transvaal.

1990   Photographs in Spain. Selects photographs to accompany a text by Willie Morris, which are published together in *Faulkner's Mississippi*.

KENYA, 1980

BIBLIOGRAPHY

BOOKS:
William Eggleston's Guide, with an essay by John Szarkowski,
The Museum of Modern Art, New York, 1976.
The Democratic Forest, with an introduction by Eudora Welty, London
and New York, 1989.

BOOKS CONTAINING PHOTOGRAPHS BY EGGLESTON:
Mirrors and Windows, John Szarkowski, The Museum of Modern Art,
New York, 1978.
American Images, New Work by Twenty Contemporary Photographers,
edited by Renato Danese, New York, 1979.
The New Color Photography, Sally Eauclaire, New York, 1981.
Annie on Camera, New York, 1982.
Elvis at Graceland, Memphis, 1983.
New Color/New Work, Sally Eauclaire, New York, 1984.
True Stories, David Byrne, New York and London, 1986.
American Independents, Sally Eauclaire, New York, 1987.
Faulkner's Mississippi, with a text by Willie Morris, Birmingham,
Alabama, 1991.
Rythm Oil, Stanley Booth, London and New York, 1991.

ARTIST'S BOOKS:
Election Eve, with a preface by Lloyd Fonvielle, 100 chromogenic
coupler prints in two volumes, published in an edition of five by
Caldecot Chubb, New York, 1977.
Morals of Vision, eight chromogenic coupler prints, published in an
edition of 15 by Caldecot Chubb, New York, 1978.
Flowers, twelve chromogenic coupler prints, published in an edition
of approximately 20 by Caldecot Chubb, New York, 1978.
Wedgwood Blue, fifteen chromogenic coupler prints, published in an
edition of 20 by Caldecot Chubb.

PORTFOLIOS:
14 Pictures, fourteen dye-transfer prints, published by Julien
Hohenberg, distributed by Harry H. Lunn Jnr., Washington D.C.,
1974.
Seven, seven chromogenic coupler prints, published by Caldecot
Chubb, New York, 1979.

Troubled Waters, fifteen dye-transfer prints, published by Caldecot
Chubb, New York, 1980.
Southern Suite, ten dye-transfer prints, published by Lunn Gallery,
Washington, D.C., 1981.
William Eggleston's Graceland, eleven dye-transfer prints, published by
Middendorf Gallery, Washington, D.C., 1984.

ARTICLES AND ESSAYS ON EGGLESTON'S WORK:
John Szarkowski, 'Photography: A Different Kind of Art', *New York
Times Sunday Magazine*, 13 April 1975.
Douglas Davis, 'New Frontiers in Color', *Newsweek*, 19 April 1976.
Hilton Kramer, 'Art: Focus on Photo Shows', *New York Times*,
28 May 1976.
Julia Scully, 'Seeing Pictures', *Modern Photography*, August 1976.
Max Kozloff, 'How to Mystify Color Photography', *Artforum*,
November 1976.
Ingrid Sischy, 'Matters of Record', *Artforum*, February 1983.
Mark Haworth-Booth, 'William Eggleston: Colour Photographs
from the American South', exhibition catalogue, Victoria and Albert
Museum, London, August 1983.
Mark Holborn, 'Color Codes', *Aperture 96*, Fall 1984.
J. Richard Gruber, 'William Eggleston's Early Black and White
Photography', exhibition catalogue, Memphis Brooks Museum,
1986.
Mark Holborn, 'William Eggleston: Democracy and Chaos',
Artforum, Summer 1988.
Charles Hagen, 'An Interview with William Eggleston', *Aperture 115*,
Summer 1989.
Andy Grundberg, book review of *The Democratic Forest*, *New York
Times*, 3 December 1989.
Malcolm Jones Jnr., 'Translating Ideas into Color', *Newsweek*,
1 January 1990.
Walter Hopps, 'Los Alamos – a fragment', *Grand Street 36*, New York,
1990.
Carole Thompson, 'William Eggleston: Seen & Unseen', *The Print
Collector's Newsletter*, vol.XXI-5, Nov-Dec, 1990.
Richard B. Woodward, 'Memphis Beau', *Vanity Fair*, October 1991.

THE TRANSVAAL, 1989

ACKNOWLEDGMENTS

The publication and exhibition *Ancient and Modern* is possible due to the great freedom granted to us by William Eggleston himself, and with the support provided by Carol Brown and her colleagues at Barbican Art Gallery, with the publishing commitment of David Godwin and Jonathan Cape Ltd., and with the editorial advice of Jenny Cottom. We are most grateful for the thorough assistance of Kip Peterson and the staff of the Memphis Brooks Museum of Art. We are also particularly grateful for the assistance and co-operation of Rosa Eggleston, Deborah Bell, Caldecot Chubb, Walter Hopps, Harry H. Lunn Jnr., Marie Martin, Peter T. Joseph and David Bonderman, David Byrne and Ingrid Sischy.

M.H.